COLOUR ME THINGS THAT GO

Buster Books

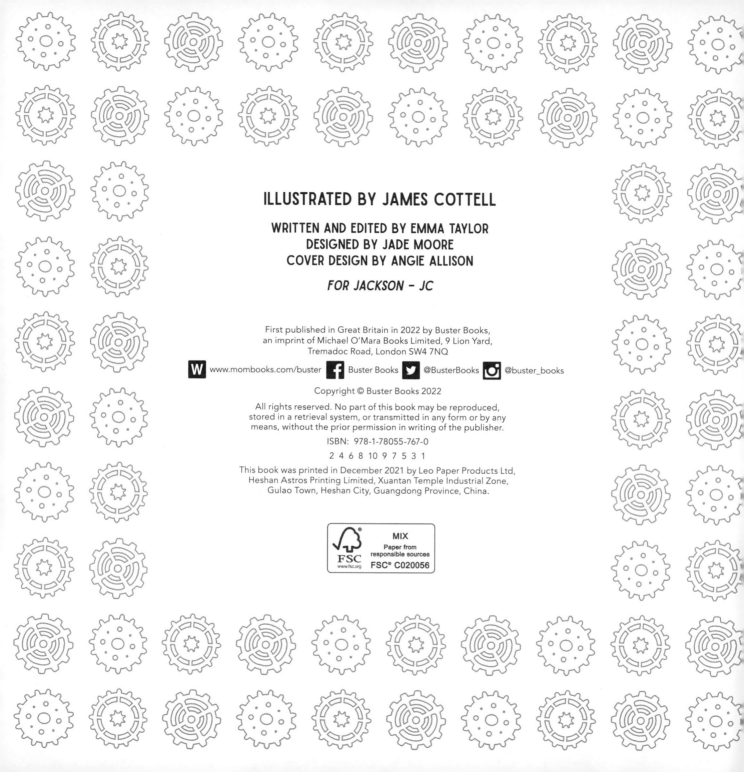

ILLUSTRATED BY JAMES COTTELL

WRITTEN AND EDITED BY EMMA TAYLOR
DESIGNED BY JADE MOORE
COVER DESIGN BY ANGIE ALLISON

FOR JACKSON – JC

First published in Great Britain in 2022 by Buster Books,
an imprint of Michael O'Mara Books Limited, 9 Lion Yard,
Tremadoc Road, London SW4 7NQ

W www.mombooks.com/buster **f** Buster Books **🐦** @BusterBooks **📷** @buster_books

ISBN: 978-1-78055-767-0

2 4 6 8 10 9 7 5 3 1

This book was printed in December 2021 by Leo Paper Products Ltd,
Heshan Astros Printing Limited, Xuantan Temple Industrial Zone,
Gulao Town, Heshan City, Guangdong Province, China.

MIX
Paper from
responsible sources
FSC® C020056
www.fsc.org

ABOUT THIS BOOK

This book is packed with all of your favourite things that go, from high-flying helicopters and jumbo jets to super-fast racing cars and speedboats.

Next to every picture is a fun fact to discover as you colour.

So grab your pens and pencils and get colouring!

SUBMARINE

A submarine is a type of boat that goes underwater.
The record for the deepest dive by a submarine is held by
American explorer Victor Vescovo, who travelled to the bottom of
the Mariana Trench in the Pacific Ocean – a depth of nearly
11 kilometres (7 miles). That's deeper than the height of
Mount Everest, the tallest mountain in the world.

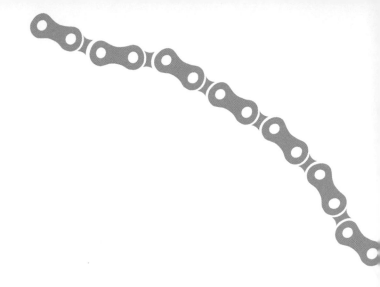

POLICE CAR

These speedy vehicles help the police to reach the scene of
a crime quickly. A police car has flashing lights and a siren, which the
police use to warn other drivers and pedestrians when they're in a hurry.

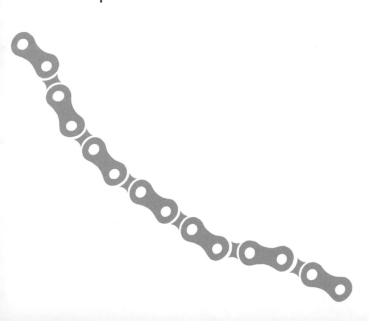

JUMBO JET

The Boeing 747 is often called the 'Jumbo Jet' because it is so big. These planes have a wingspan of about 68 metres (220 feet) – that's the same as five buses all in a line. The newest model can carry 467 passengers.

GO-KART

Go-karts are small vehicles with four wheels. Special go-karts, called Superkarts, can reach speeds of more than 260 kilometres per hour (160 miles per hour). That's almost as fast as a helicopter.

GONDOLA

A gondola is a type of rowing boat that is mainly used on the canals of Venice, Italy. It is steered by a person called a 'gondolier'. Gondoliers train at a special school where they have to take exams in rowing and swimming.

BICYCLE

These popular, two-wheeled vehicles are used for transport, exercise and racing. In 1935, Fred A. Birchmore from America travelled the globe by bicycle and wore out seven sets of tyres on his journey.

TRAM

A tram is a vehicle that runs along tracks in a road.
The world's largest tram network is in Melbourne, Australia,
and is 250 kilometres (155 miles) long.

MOTORBOAT

A motorboat is a type of small boat which can travel at over 160 kilometres per hour (100 miles per hour). It is often used for sports, such as fishing, swimming, diving, water skiing and racing.

SPACE SHUTTLE

The Space Shuttle was a type of spacecraft used by NASA
for carrying people and cargo into space between 1981 and 2011.
It had rocket boosters attached to its sides, which gave the craft the fuel
and power it needed to lift off from the ground.

DOG SLED

Sleds are small land vehicles that can slide over snow and ice.
Sleds pulled by dogs have been around for thousands of years and
were first made by people living in the Arctic. Sled dogs have
two coats of fur to keep them warm and thick pads on their
paws to protect them from the ice.

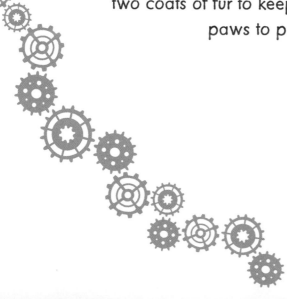

MONSTER TRUCK

The mighty monster truck is a vehicle that is custom-built for competitions. It's a heavy truck with huge wheels, and some models can weigh more than 5,000 kilograms (5 tons). That's heavier than an adult hippopotamus.

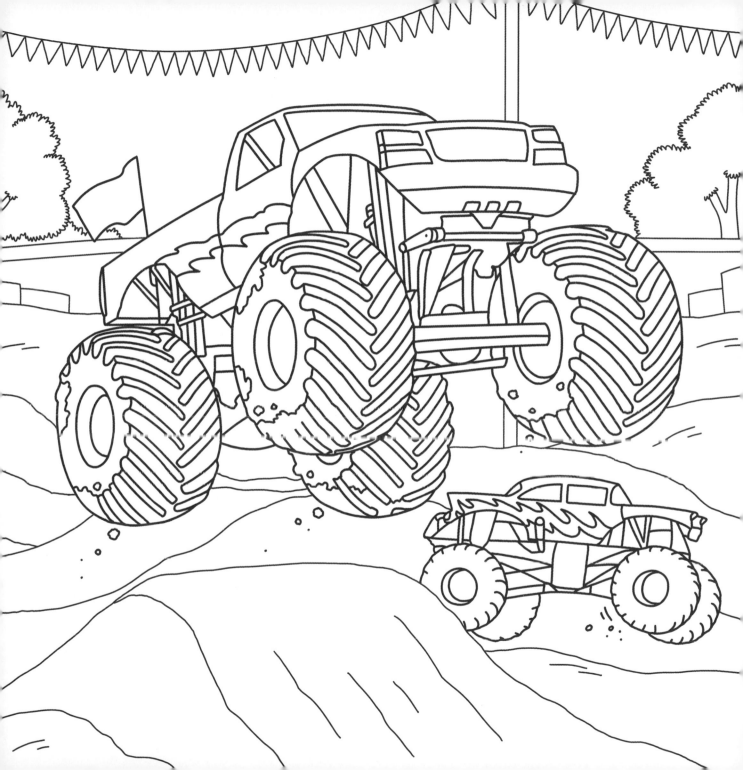

DID YOU KNOW?

Modern diggers can work as quickly as 20 construction workers put together. They are powerful, heavy machines and can weigh up to 1 million kilograms (1,100 tons). That's heavier than nine blue whales, the largest animals on the planet.

CRUISE SHIP

Cruise ships are like floating hotels that take people on holiday. The largest cruise ships have swimming pools, cinemas and lots of restaurants. Some of the biggest can carry over 5,000 passengers and reach the same height as a 16-storey building.

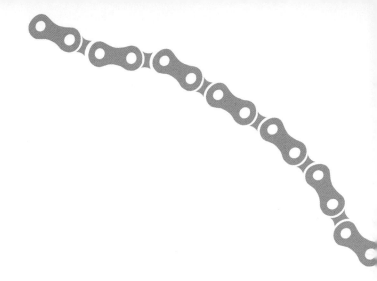

ELECTRIC CAR

Electric cars run on electricity instead of fuel made from oil.
Much like a smartphone, they have rechargeable batteries. They are
much better for the environment as they create very little air pollution.

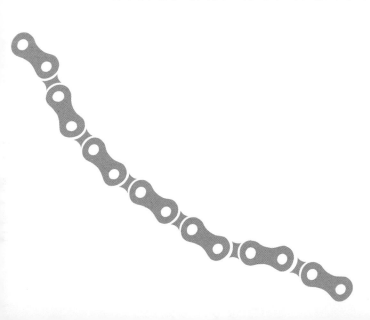

HOT-AIR BALLOON

The world's first ever aircraft was a hot-air balloon. In 1783,
a duck, a sheep and a cockerel were sent into the air to prove that
the balloon's design was safe to travel in. They survived the flight,
which confirmed it was safe for use by humans.

MOTORCYCLE

Motorcycles are two-wheeled vehicles powered by an engine.
The world's fastest motorcycles can reach top speeds of
over 650 kilometres per hour (400 miles per hour) – that's
twice as fast as a sports car.

TRAIN

Trains can travel quickly across long distances and are used for carrying people and cargo. The United States has the longest railway network in the world, stretching about 150,000 kilometres (90,000 miles). That's the same as three and a half trips around the Earth.

KAYAK

Kayaks are around 4,000 years old and were invented by people living in the Arctic. They were originally made for fishing and hunting, but now they are mostly used for fun and sightseeing.

SNOW PLOUGH

A snow plough is used to clear snow from the ground to make roads safer for drivers. Some snow ploughs have extra features, such as sweeper brooms and blowers to help clear the snow.

GLIDER

Gliders have two very long, narrow wings,
which allow them to stay in the air for hours at a time.
They have no engine of their own so they are usually towed into
the air by a propeller-driven plane in order to take off.

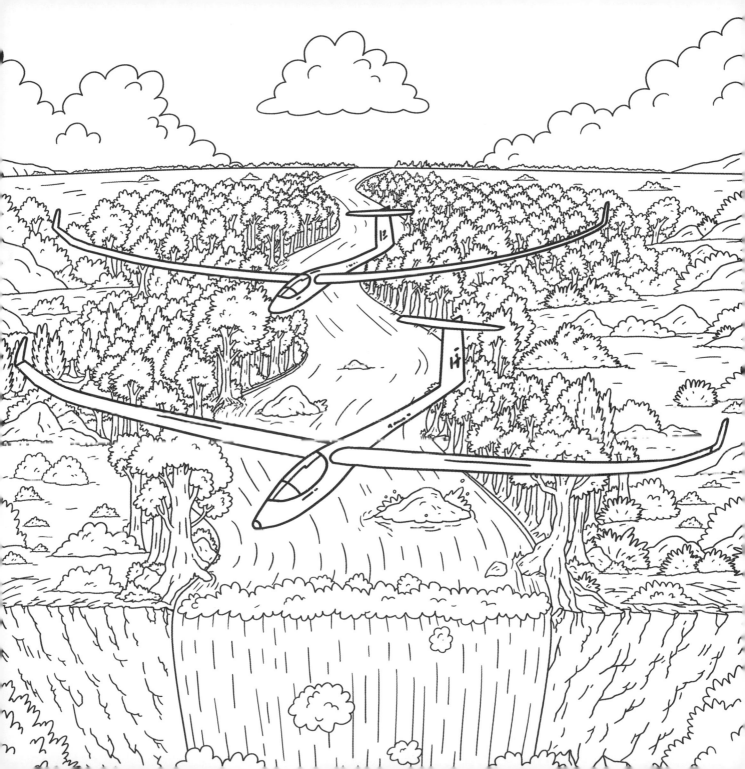

FIRE TRUCK

Fire trucks carry equipment for putting out fires, such as water hoses and ladders. Much like police cars, they have flashing lights and sirens which they use for emergencies. Some fire trucks are fitted with special ladders, which can reach fires that are many storeys high.

HORSE AND CARRIAGE

Horse-drawn carriages have been around for thousands of years. Before the invention of cars, they were used to transport people and cargo and were even used for racing. Today, they are used as transportation for weddings and other special occasions, as well as sightseeing.

HOVERCRAFT

Hovercrafts are vehicles that move about on a cushion of air.
They can travel over land, water, mud, ice and most other
smooth surfaces. They are often used as ferries to carry people,
cargo and sometimes even other vehicles.

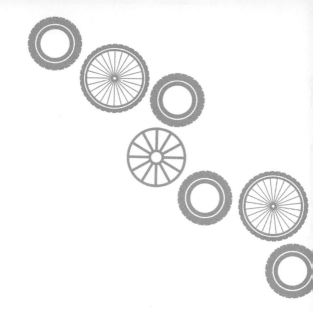

RACING CAR

There are lots of different types of racing car, but Formula One cars are the fastest. They can travel at speeds of more than 360 kilometres per hour (220 miles per hour). That's about as fast as a high-speed train.

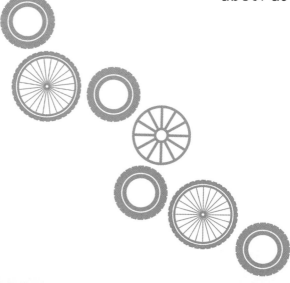

SCOOTER

The scooter has been a popular kids' toy since the early 1900s.
The record for the fastest mile ridden on a scooter is held by
Christian Roberto López Rodríguez from Spain, who completed
the mile in 6 minutes and 15.81 seconds.

AIRSHIP

Airships are big balloons that are able to fly because they are
filled with a gas that is lighter than air. Early airships were powered
by steam engines but modern airships have electric motors.
Today, they are used for sightseeing and filming.

RICKSHAW BICYCLES

Rickshaw bicycles are used all over the world as an important mode of short-distance transportation. They are often painted in bright colours or with eye-catching designs to attract customers.

ICE-CREAM TRUCK

Ice-cream trucks can often be seen throughout the spring and summer months near parks or beaches. Crewe in England holds the Guinness World Record for the longest ice-cream truck parade, which was made up of 84 trucks.

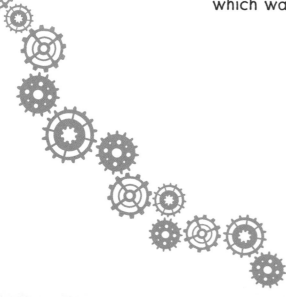

CARGO SHIP

A cargo ship transports all kinds of goods inside containers. Some of the biggest cargo ships measure almost 400 metres (1,300 feet) in length. That's bigger than the height of the Empire State Building in New York, United States of America.

TRACTOR

A tractor is a piece of farming machinery, which can be used to pull along tools or trailers. It is a big, noisy vehicle and some tractors have wheels that are taller than an adult.

CAMPERVAN

Campervans are specially made vehicles used for transport, as well as cooking and sleeping. When going on holiday, some people might choose to stay in a campervan instead of a hotel. Some models have fridges, televisions and even showers.

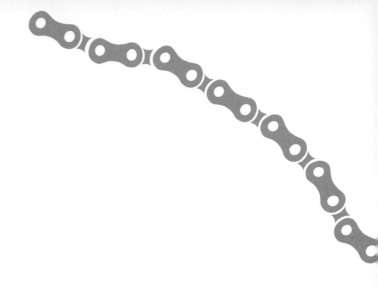

CEMENT TRUCK

Cement trucks combine cement, sand, gravel and water to make concrete, which is stored inside a big spinning barrel on top of the truck. Large cement trucks can carry around 18,100 kilograms (20 tons) of concrete. That's about the weight of three Tyrannosaurus rexes!

SAILING BOAT

A sailing boat uses the wind in its sails to move, but some also have engines. Sailing boats can travel long distances, sometimes even around the world. The first person to sail around the world by themselves was Joshua Slocum from Canada, who began the journey in 1895 and finished it in 1898.

CABLE CAR

A cable car is a carriage that hangs from and is moved
by a cable. It's often used to transport people in areas where there
are lots of mountains. The highest cable car in the world is in
Merida, Venezuela, and is over 4,760 metres (15,600 feet) high.
That's half the height of Mount Everest.

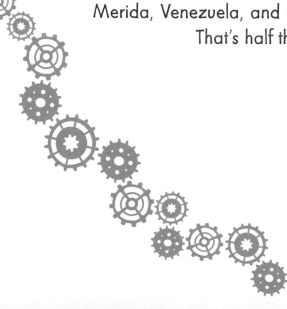

FREIGHT TRAIN

Freight trains are used to carry cargo over long distances. They are often very long and made up of many individual wagons that are all linked together. One record-breaking freight train in Australia contained over 680 wagons and was 7.3 kilometres (4.5 miles) long.

MONOPLANE

Monoplanes have a single pair of wings.
The first monoplane was built in 1906 and its design is
still used in almost all modern high-speed aircrafts.

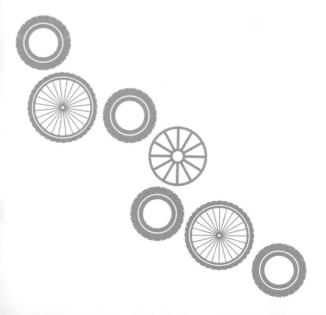

DID YOU KNOW?

From tiny screws and seatbelts to steering wheels and tyres,
the average car is made up of around 30,000 separate parts.

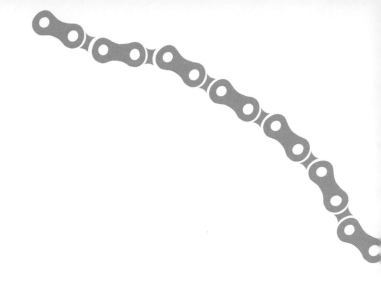

FERRY BOAT

This type of boat is used to take people, vehicles and cargo across water. It is estimated that ferries transport over 2 billion people and over 250 million vehicles every year. Some remote places in the world can only be reached by ferry, as they don't have any roads, railways or airports.

AMBULANCE

Ambulances carry sick or injured people to hospital.
As well as having a siren and flashing lights, they are painted in bright,
reflective colours so that they can be easily spotted on busy roads.

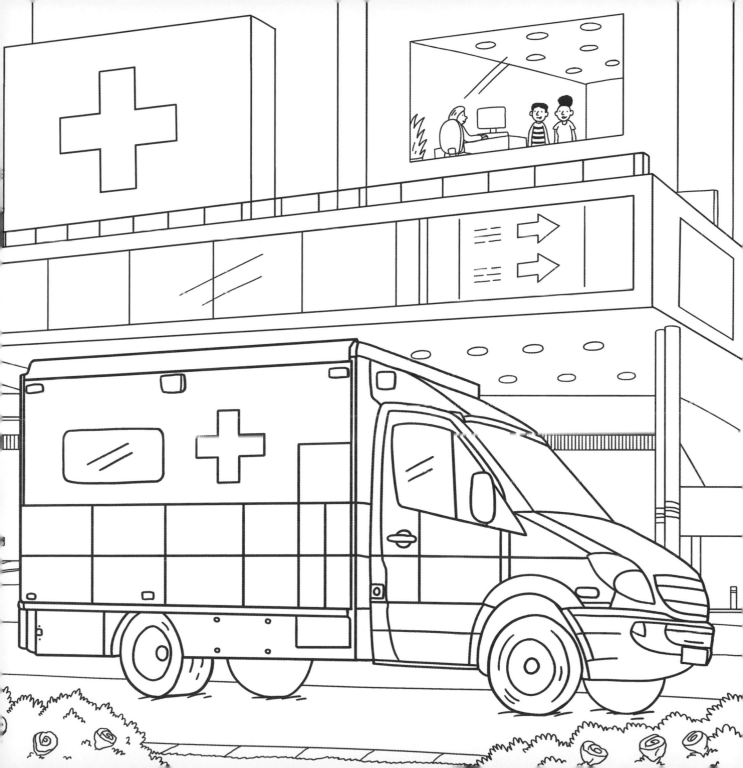

BUS

This big-wheeled vehicle is a type of public transport
used to carry many passengers from one place to another.
In the early 1900s, buses were developed to offer
a more flexible alternative to trams.

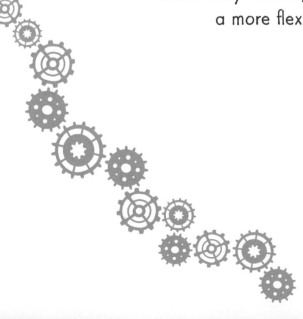

BIPLANE

A biplane is a type of aircraft with two wings, placed one above the other. The world's first successful motor-operated plane was a biplane, which was built by the Wright brothers in 1903.

EXCAVATOR

Excavators are strong vehicles used for digging and moving heavy objects. The first excavator was the steam shovel, which was made around 200 years ago. This steam-powered machine used chains, pulleys and gears to dig through the earth.

HELICOPTER

Helicopters are a type of aircraft that are lifted and propelled
by blades. Unlike a plane, they can spin around and hover in the air.
They are often used for rescue missions, as they can fly almost anywhere.

FORKLIFT TRUCK

These trucks are used for lifting heavy loads and moving them short distances. The world record for the heaviest load ever lifted by a forklift truck is 90,000 kilograms (99 tons). That's as heavy as 15 African elephants.

HOUSEBOAT

Houseboats are boats that have been built for people
to use as homes. The canals of Amsterdam in the Netherlands
are home to around 2,500 houseboats, many of which
are anchored in the city centre.

SEA PLANE

A sea plane is an aircraft that has floats so that it can take off from, and land on, water. Sea planes are mostly used in places where there are lots of islands that have little space to build big runways.